Small Houses

Lila Gault & Jeffrey Weiss

Photography by David Leach

Additional photos by: Jon Elliott, Michael Kanouff

WARNER BOOKS

A Warner Communications Company

 A Warner Communications Company

WARNER BOOKS EDITION
Copyright © 1980 by Lila Gault and Jeffrey Weiss
All rights reserved.
Warner Books, Inc., 75 Rockefeller Plaza, New York, N.Y. 10019
        A Warner Communications Company
Printed in the United States of America
First printing: May 1980
10   9   8   7   6   5   4   3   2   1

LIbrary of Congress Cataloging in Publication Data

Gault, Lila.
   Small houses.

   1. Small houses—United states. I. Friedman-Weiss,
Jeffrey, joint author. II. Title.
NA7205.G38   728.3'7'0873   80-267
ISBN 0-446-97346-7

Many thanks to the owners and
architects who let us explore their
small houses.

Len Hughes Andrus and Mary O'Hara-
   Devereaux
James Cutler
Bill and Mary Earngey
Ron Gold
Frances Grill
Joyce Nordfors and Associates
Thomas Kazas and Teresa Lynch
Chad Kirk AIA
Barry and Linda Meyers
Jeffrey Milstein, Architect
John and Arlene Noble
Pearl Reed
Douglas Shaw/Struktures Inc.
Barbara Silverberg
SolArc Energy Design
Daniel and Barbara Solomon
Richard and Margaret Storch
George Suppes
Les Walker

Book and Cover Design
by Carl Berkowitz

Introduction

As we enter the 1980s, America is discovering the beauty and satisfaction of small. Small cars fill the highways and small families are rapidly becoming the rule. But perhaps the most dramatic evidence of the trend toward thinking small is the popularity of the well-designed, painstakingly crafted small house.

In a world of shrinking resources and double-digit inflation, the demand for small houses is obviously practical. A small house uses less energy from conventional sources and is often a showcase for alternative sources such as passive or active solar heating systems or wood heat from a single well-placed stove. Smaller houses seldom require as much cash to build, renovate, or restore as do larger dwellings and usually need less maintenance as well. Although the practical aspects of a small house may provide the initial attraction for many prospective residents, those considerations are often simply the beginning.

Small houses today are often built or restored with imaginative design and elegant decor, which historically the typical small house lacked. Although many current owners of small houses are budget conscious, they are often not as severely limited by lack of money as were small-house builders and buyers in previous generations. Today the small-house owner is often able to invest savings that accumulate by limiting overall size throughout the house. These houses boast exquisite finish detail, quality craftsmanship, and handsome furnishings that are often eliminated in a house dedicated to the creation of maximum floor space.

Most of the houses in this book contain less than 1200 square feet. Some are simply a single room that serves successfully as an entire house, with the focus on certain activities in specific areas of the room. Other houses are a series of small rooms, annexed and arranged in one, two, and even three-story configurations. Many give the appearance of greater than actual size by using such design elements as high ceilings and oversized windows, while others emphasize the coziness and intimacy that are implicit in limited floor space.

These houses differ greatly in design, age, and style. Some are brand new; others are quite historic. There are carefully planned restorations that have been researched and executed in precise and authentic detail. Some maintain the integrity of a classic exterior but have redesigned interior space to provide up-to-date comfort and convenience.

While substantial savings in construction and operation costs can be realized in the well-designed small house, the cost per square foot of residential construction makes virtually any house a major investment. According to a recent edition of the Boeckh Building Valuation Manual, the cost of a very basic 1200-square-foot single-story frame house with no basement is $29,540 in Boston. The same house would cost $30,858 to build in Chicago and $31,913 in Seattle.

Work together more closely in order to stretch the building dollar. One popular solution is to design a single structure for use both residentially and commercially. Even some of the smallest houses include a studio or office, and others a rental unit. But whether it is a multipurpose structure or one that is strictly residential, the small house is increasingly attractive to most lending institutions because of its strong current market value and excellent resale potential.

Even state and local governments are recognizing the practicality and appeal of the small house. Certain requirements in building codes are being revised—for example, a reduction in necessary minimum room size-—without compromising standards of health and safety.

We are grateful to the owners, architects, and builders whose small houses we have explored throughout this past year. We found a variety of styles, intentions, and ideas from Chester County, Pennsylvania, to Bainbridge Island, Washington, that is evidence of imagination, hard work, and good sense. As a result, we have proof that small can truly be beautiful.

Lila Gault
Jeffrey Weiss

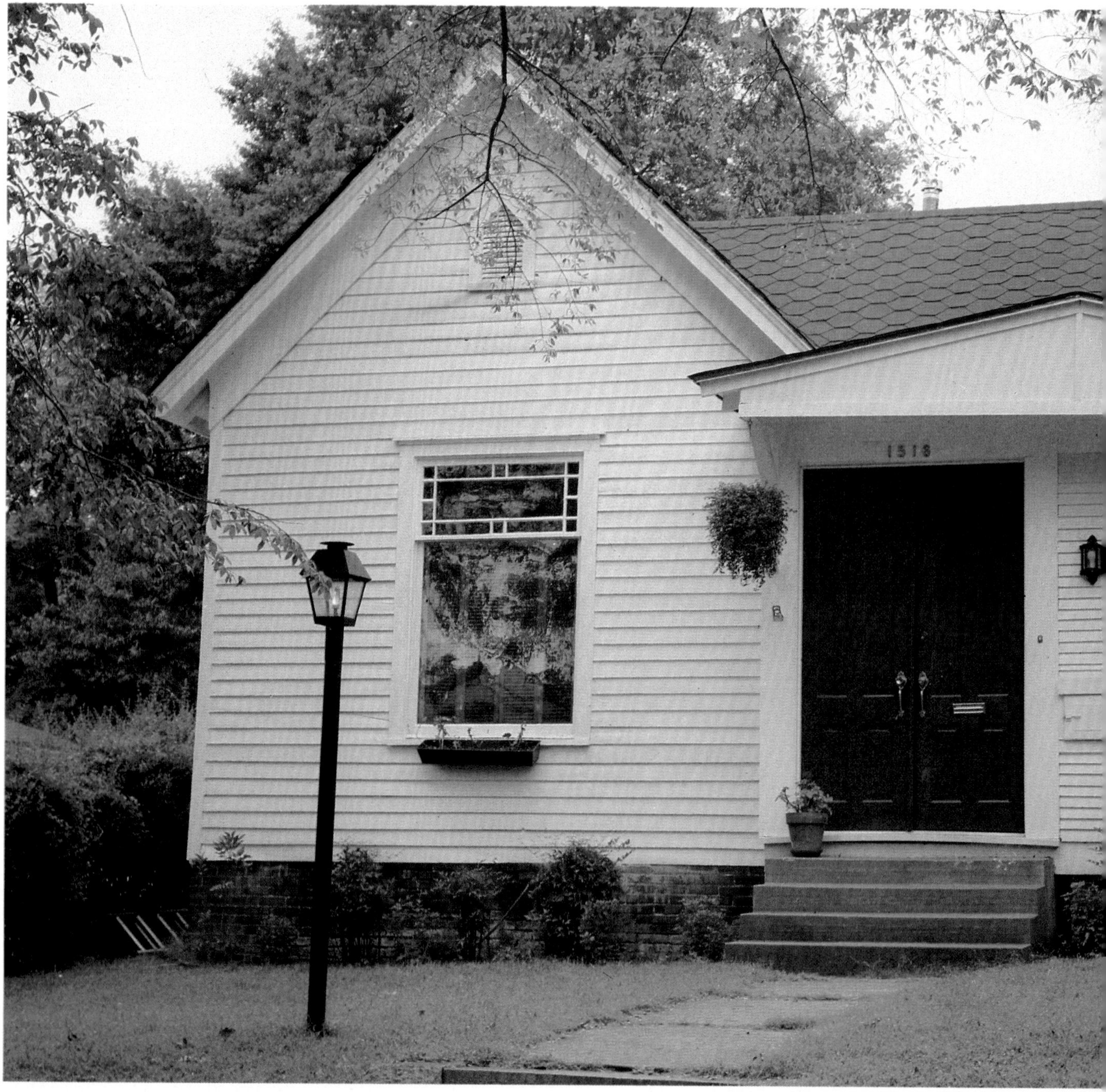
1518

The owners of this restored Victorian cottage came to Little Rock, Arkansas, in 1977 in search of a small house to bring back to life. She was a veteran of two major residential restorations in Massachusetts and Maine. Together they had built a one-room cabin in the Ozark Mountains, using only hand tools.

They combed the city for a neglected small house and found an appropriate challenge for their carpentry skills and eye for historic design in the then-reviving downtown residential area of Governors' Mansion. The house was purchased for $14,500 in early 1978. Eighteen months and nearly $12,000 later, the restoration was complete.

The house, built in 1881, had been used as a church in recent years and had been radically altered from its original three-room plan. In order to eliminate the effects of years of careless remodeling and re-create the simple comfort of a modest Victorian home, the owners had to gut much of the interior. They then designed a flowing floor plan with several large rooms to replace much of the original scheme.

An original wall was rebuilt to create a living room and dining room from a single large area that the church had used for meetings. Other interior walls were eliminated or relocated in order to

enlarge the bathroom, for example, and create a large country kitchen.

Many recycled materials were used to save money, as well as put authentic late-nineteenth-century detail throughout the house. The owners spent several months at auctions and in second-hand stores, buying doors, windows, hardware, lighting, and plumbing fixtures. Countless hours were subsequently devoted to stripping, polishing, and repairing these treasures for use in the house.

Despite its urban location, this small house is rich in classic details that are often found in country farmhouses. Wide oak floorboards complement the refinished cypress and pine flooring that remained from the original house. There is a simple tiled hearth for the wood stove in the kitchen. The windows, doors, and baseboards are trimmed with painted wide pine boards.

The country feeling is enhanced by the collection of pine and oak antique furniture that the owners brought to this house from previous residences. In contrast, there are several contemporary watercolors on walls throughout the house. The house, furniture, and paintings blend successfully as different, complementary expressions of simple design, good taste, and hard work.

Ron Gold

This small handcrafted house, located in Woodstock, New York, reflects the architectural imagination and religious enthusiasm of its designer/builder. It is entirely constructed from windows, beams, flooring, and other characteristic building materials that were collected and salvaged from local abandoned churches. The house was designed to use the recycled materials in an aesthetically pleasing, yet spiritually meaningful, manner. As a result, the building is really a small chapel as well as a small house.

A simple plan was drawn to include a sharply sloping roof and seven massive oak beams for structural support. There are two large rooms on the main floor of the 400-square-foot house and a small bedroom and bath on the second floor. Each room receives maximum natural light through several large windows. A tower with windows on all sides is located over the stairway to ensure adequate daylight in that area.

One of the downstairs rooms is a study and the other a multipurpose living area and kitchen. The wood-burning airtight stove, located in a corner of the living room on a brick hearth, is used for cooking, heating water, and heating the entire house as well. The house is lit by several wall-mounted oil

lamps, since there is no electricity. Water is carried into the house in buckets from the nearby well for cooking use or filling a basin and pitcher in the bathroom. A chemical toilet provides effective sanitary waste disposal.

The house is sited on three heavily wooded acres divided into quadrants by two large streams. There are several hand-built footbridges over the streams, a

shingled roof over the well, and a series of rock walls. It took the builder less than a year to complete the house and then add the final touches in thoughtful landscape detail.

The designer/builder of this remarkable house left Woodstock several years ago. The house was bought by a close friend, who uses it on weekends throughout the year and treasures its handcrafted elegance.

"I see this house as a big toy," says the architect/builder/owner of this 640-square-foot residence in Woodstock, New York. "Most of the cabinet work in the bedrooms, kitchen, and office was prefitted, painted, and then installed like dollhouse furniture. In addition, since I like to see how buildings are put together, I emphasized the structure of this house by painting it green."

This small house sits on a heavily wooded site beside a broad and active stream. In order to bring as much of the view and sound of the stream into the house as possible, the architect stretched the house in a linear plan with rooms and large windows on the stream side and a hallway on the entry side. The opposing facades are also dramatically different. The entry side features decorative shingles, a sloping roof, fancy porch railing, and brick walk. The stream side of the house is sleek and spare with large areas of glass, a flat porch deck, flat roof, and the surrounding natural landscape.

The house was begun in the spring of 1977 and completed one year later. The architect worked alone as the builder. The total cost of building materials, a well, and a septic system was $20,000. The architect/builder and his eight-year-old son lived in the house while it was under construction.

"The house is small enough so that I could build and rebuild certain parts of it when necessary, almost as if it was a large sculpture. I rebuilt one window four times until the light was absolutely right. The shelves in the kitchen and the desk in the office were rebuilt once and redesigned twice until they were efficient." Such perfection would be difficult to achieve and sustain in a larger house.

Father and son enjoy maximum privacy! Their bedrooms are located at opposite ends of the house. In addition, sleeping accommodations for guests are in two small lofts that can be reached by ladders from the first floor. The lofts are separated from the office on the second floor by a large skylight located over the dining area.

All of the furniture in the house, except the dining table and chairs, is built into each room to maximize usable floor space and eliminate costly, time-consuming maintenance. The central location of an airtight wood-burning stove is further evidence of the efficiency and careful design of this house. The stove heats the entire house satisfactorily throughout the year, and a back-up electrical system is rarely in use.

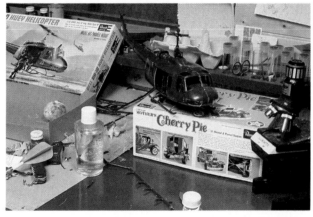

Barry and Linda Meyers

"We rarely feel any lack of privacy or the need for more actual space," the owners agreed, "because psychologically, this structure is really two different houses." This 1200-square-foot house on Bainbridge Island, Washington, began as a small cabin which the owners built themselves in the summer of 1977. They were restricted at the time by a severely limited budget and built the cabin as a house in which they could live for years if necessary.

The cabin, which has become the main activity center in the completed residence, has a kitchen, bathroom, pantry/storage area, and a large sleeping loft. In 1978, when time and money allowed, a sleeping wing with two large bedrooms, a bathroom, and storage area were added. Both ends of the house are connected by a bridge that has hemlock decking on the floor.

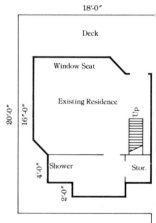

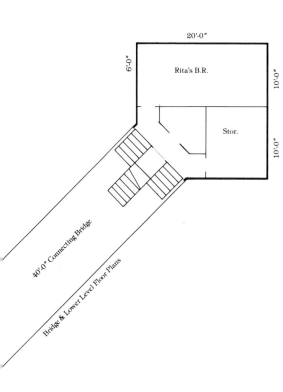

20'-0"

6'-0"

Rita's B.R.

10'-0"

10'-0"

Stor.

40'-0" Connecting Bridge

Bridge & Lower Level Floor Plans

Roof Line

Corrugated fiberglass panels on the roof permit outdoor use throughout the year.

The design of this small house was determined in part by the site and also by the owners' interest in an architecturally innovative plan. The building site is a natural clearing in a second-growth deciduous forest that is 100 feet in diameter and is bisected by a large ravine. A house that spread across the ravine with a steep roof to shed forest debris seemed to be the best solution for the demanding location.

The house has been handcrafted by the owners with help from talented friends and is full of beautifully executed, thoughtful details, such as a tiled shower in the bathroom with a Dutch door that opens outside onto a small private deck. Much of the cabinet, door, and window hardware is brass. There are mahogany magazine and towel racks in each bathroom. Each end of the house has a pyramidal skylight that helps assure maximum use of natural light.

This house offers more storage space than many houses of similar size because the owners made adequate storage an important priority. Each second-floor bedroom has a custom-designed platform bed with built-in dressers underneath. There are cabinets tucked into traditionally wasted spaces—for example, under the eaves in the sleeping loft—as well as rooms reserved especially for storage on both sides of the house.

A small parlor stove heats the original cabin. The electric baseboard heating system in the sleeping wing is rarely in use in the mild Northwest climate. Although the size of the house makes it comparatively energy-efficient, the owners plan to increase the efficiency with eventual installation of a solar energy system.

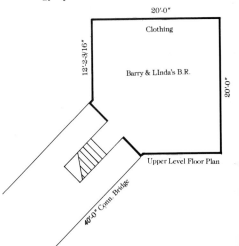

20'-0"

Clothing

13'-2-3/16"

Barry & LInda's B.R.

20'-0"

40'-0" Conn. Bridge

Upper Level Floor Plan

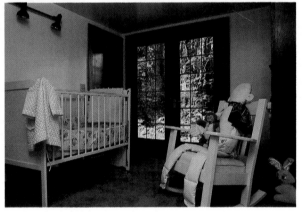

This 1400-square-foot house, located in the hills above Oakland, California, is a study in unconventional geometric design, using recycled building materials. The dramatic curves of the hyperbolic roof work in graceful contrast to the angular sidewalls, irregular windows, and diagonal redwood siding to create constant visual interest inside and outside of this unique small house.

The interior is divided into three separate levels, which appear almost continuous because of ample use of open space. The living room is on the lowest level and is appended by

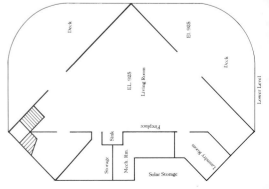

two large semicircular decks, as is the dining room and kitchen that is located above. Each deck is reached through a large sliding-glass panel door that has been framed with massive redwood timbers and mounted on barn-door runners. A curved stairway leads to a bedroom on the uppermost level.

Up to 70 percent of the energy requirements for the house is provided by an active solar system that includes collector panels on the roof over the adjacent carport and storage tanks beneath the house. A back-up gas system is necessary, however, to provide adequate heat and hot water when the skies turn gray. In addition a fireplace in the living room provides heat in cooler months.

The sharply sloping 1/4 acre site has given the owner an interesting landscaping challenge. She has planted a low-maintenance, drought-resistant variety of native California and Australian plants, including manzanita, ceonothis, grezillea, and protea, as well as a small vegetable garden.

The house is furnished with a

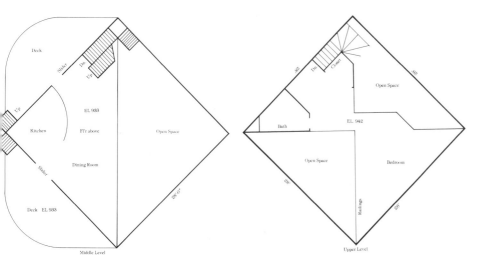

Deck

Slider

Dn

Up

Up

Kitchen

EL 933

Fl'r above

Slider

Dining Room

Open Space

Deck EL 933

26'-0"

Middle Level

Dn

Closet

40°

Open Space

90°

Bath

EL 942

Open Space

Bedroom

90°

Railings

40°

90°

Upper Level

stylish combination of tables made from recycled wooden machinery molds, elegant Chinese rosewood antiques, and several very contemporary designer pieces. Ceremonial masks and other forms of primitive art from Africa, Bali, and Northwest American Indians provide decorative accents.

"I have an extraordinary sense of freedom in this house," says the owner after two and a half years in residence, "because of the way in which the levels interact. There is a feeling of unlimited space and architectural uniqueness that is rarely found in any house, much less a house that is truly small."

Some of the richest farmland in America is found in Chester County, Pennsylvania, where crop and dairy farming has been a way of life for many families since the days of William Penn. The gently rolling countryside is beginning to show signs of suburban development now, but many farms are still in operation, growing corn and wheat, raising cattle and other livestock, and providing food for kitchens in nearby cities such as Philadelphia and New York.

Many of these farms include hundreds of acres and have always been too large to be operated and overseen by a single family without help. Most farmers became dependent on reliable hired hands to run their farms and were often willing to provide a house for their workers as part of their wages. As a result, it is not unusual to find several small cabins or houses of simple design and sturdy construction near the large and often lavish brick or fieldstone farmhouses on many Chester County farms.

This small house was moved to its present site in 1928 to provide shelter for a hired hand and his family. It had been built around 1880 on a farm in a nearby county from local timber and other readily available materials.

When the present owners decided to restore the house for their own use in 1936, they began by replastering the exterior of the two-story structure in order to reduce the uncomfortable presence of indoor drafts. The

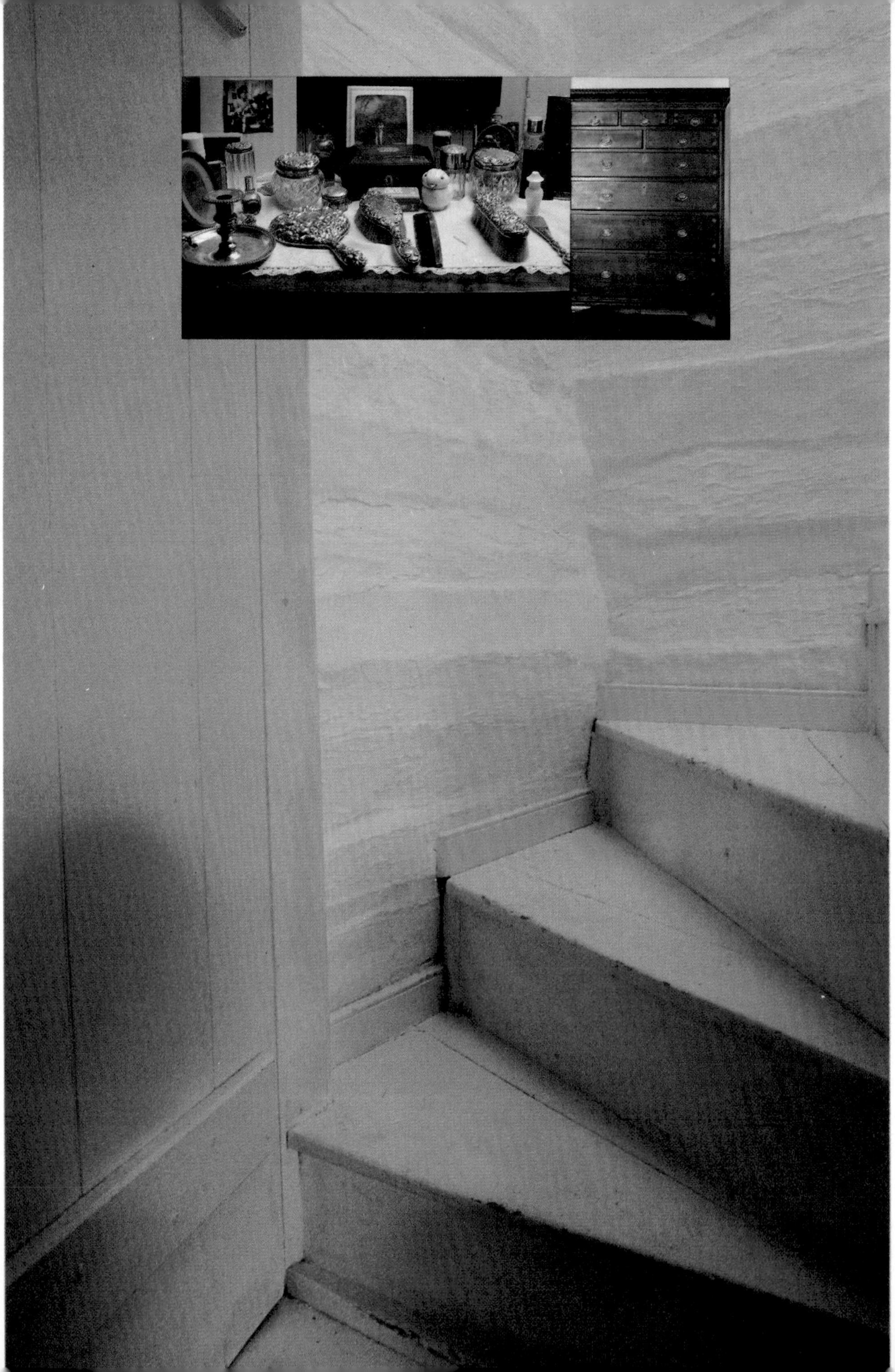

weatherizing of the cabin continued with a new cedar shingle roof, replacement of exterior door and window trim, and rehanging of the two outside doors.

After the structural repair was completed, the owners turned their attention to the five small rooms inside the house. The log walls were painted white in every room to soften their rough, uneven texture as well as to lighten the interior. The wide pine floorboards in the parlor and kitchen were refinished and the exposed beams stained dark brown. Since her family had been makers of iron hardware for several generations, the owner had accumulated a large collection of antique latches, locks, and hinges and installed several on windows and doors in this house.

She also collected American antiques, and the house is filled with pieces found in local antique shops as well as family heirlooms. The limited size of this very small house required every piece of furniture to be useful as well as decorative. That dual consideration is best seen in the standing cherry corner cupboard in the kitchen that was built around 1780 with handblown glass panels in the doors. The cupboard provides cabinet space in the tiny kitchen, as well as shelves for decorative display of the owner's fine china.

Solar Duplex, Berkeley, California, 1978 (completed). Complete design services for a two story 1,250 S.F. duplex incorporating a solar hot water system with skylights and sundecks. Insulation and solar mass wall reduce standard heating needs by 90%. Budget: $80,000.

A small house can be an ideal opportunity for the practical application of alternative energy sources. This renovated grocery store/apartment, built in 1911 on a small city lot in Berkeley, California, combines both active and passive solar energy systems to provide most of its space heating and hot water requirements. The complex, which includes a small rental unit in addition to the architect/owner's residence, is not only extremely energy efficient but more spacious and comfortable than its 1250 square feet of floor space might otherwise suggest.

The existing structure, remodeled as a duplex in 1955, presented several fundamental problems. First of all, the building completely filled its narrow 14 by 78 foot site, which eliminated a yard or any surrounding open space at street level. The duplex was little more than a series of badly lit, small rooms that had deteriorated substantially over the years.

The duplex function was maintained by the present owner, but both units were dramatically redesigned. The ceiling in the main living area of the owner's unit was raised to double height. The attic in the rental unit was opened for use as a sleeping loft. Two rooftop decks, one with a hot tub, were added to the area between the decks to ensure privacy, serve as a mount for/an active solar energy collector, and give visual height to the owner's bedroom below.

Hot water for both units and heating for the rooftop hot tub are supplied by an active solar collection system. A fiberglass-covered concrete south wall, faced inside with quarry tile, collects solar heat during the day and radiates it slowly into the rental unit at night. This passive solar system provides 95 percent of the space-heating needs for the rental apartment. The owner's unit is heated by south-facing windows and skylights and, when necessary, a heat-circulating fireplace.

The original stucco exterior has been covered with beveled redwood siding and trim that gives the duplex a contemporary but unassuming appearance. Redwood was also used to build an attractive lattice fence on the hot-tub deck for privacy from the street.

The owner's apartment is rich in simple, well-designed details, such as a long pot rack that holds large bowls, pans, and other kitchen equipment in a convenient location above the stove and sink. Plants appear throughout the house, which not only provide decoration in each room, but tie the interior together with the well-planted rooftop deck.

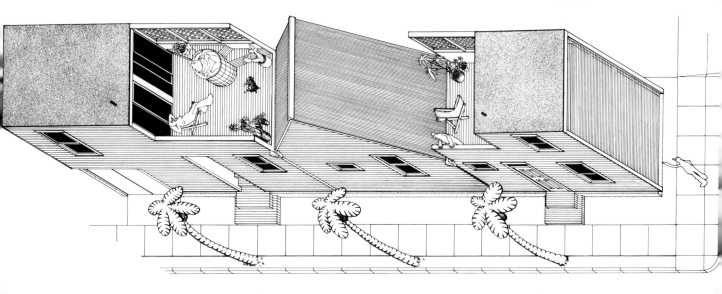

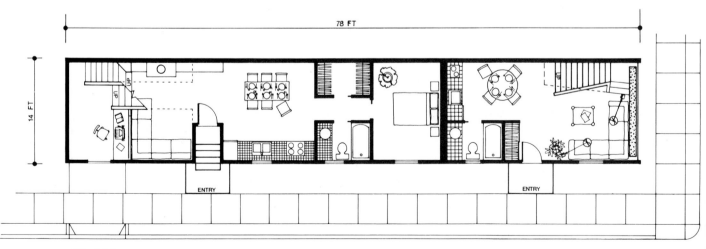

78 FT

14 FT

ENTRY

ENTRY

PLAN

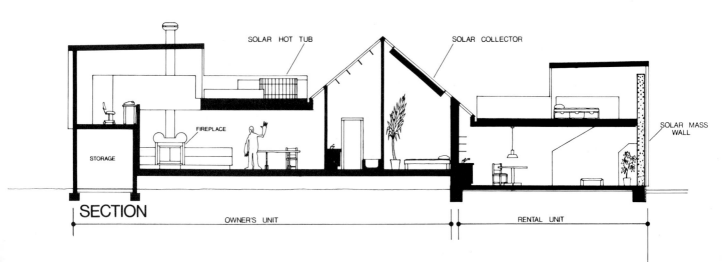

SOLAR HOT TUB

SOLAR COLLECTOR

SOLAR MASS WALL

FIREPLACE

STORAGE

SECTION

OWNER'S UNIT

RENTAL UNIT

Daniel and Barbara Solomon

This extensively remodeled
duplex in the North Beach
district of San Francisco
demonstrates both imaginative
design and dramatic engineering
rarely found in any residence,
much less a four-level building
with less than 1600 square feet.

When the architect/owner and
his family began to look for a
house to buy in the city, they
knew that they wanted a small

house. They also knew as lifelong residents of San Francisco that they wanted a view of the Bay. When they found a deteriorating two-unit duplex for sale in 1972 at a very affordable price, the rooms with a view became a potential reality.

A cross-shaped upper level was added to the existing structure in order to capture the view, create sufficient living space for the owners and their then-infant daughter, and maintain the economic attraction of the rental unit. The additional space provided a master sleeping area and a bridge to a rooftop deck and left large interior openings for natural light to fall from upper windows and skylights onto the main floor below.

The main floor was the

original upper duplex unit. This area was redesigned to accommodate a living room and centrally located dining area with a small kitchen to one side and the child's bedroom and bath, which are the only enclosed spaces in the house, at one end. The combined floor space on the main and upper floor is only 960 square feet.

In order to eliminate the need for plywood shear walls which would destroy the openness of the interior space but would satisfy provisions in the strict San Francisco building code on potential earthquake and wind forces, the architect and a structural engineer designed a steel frame to strengthen the house and meet code requirements. The frame consists of two tall narrow rectangles that were inserted through the house at the front and rear and then imbedded in concrete underneath the gargage floor. The frame was left exposed and painted tile red.

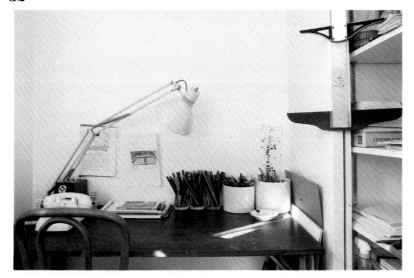

Additionally, a three-foot sideways extension of the outside wall made room for stairs to the new level, created storage space, and allowed a fireplace alcove to be built. The extensive structural renovation of the residence was time-consuming and expensive, but the entire project was completed in a little less than a year.

The interior is finished in very simple flush detail and is furnished with an eclectic combination of contemporary and period pieces. The house is used as one large open room, but no single area is as popular as the rooftop deck. The deck is thickly planted with pots of ferns and colorful annuals in season and serves as an outdoor dining area in the warm summer months.

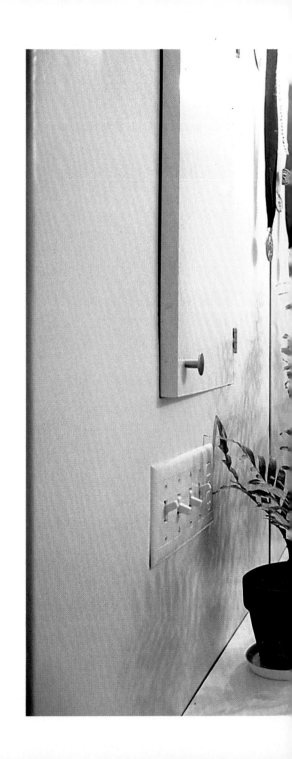

The translucent plastic roof, exposed structural stickwork, and unfinished pine on the walls, floor, and trim give a rustic yet very sophisticated appearance to this very small weekend house in Woodstock, New York. The 10 by 20 foot structure was built as a studio and workshop in 1975. A year later, it was purchased by its present owner and redesigned for all-weather use as a complete and comfortable house.

The studio was built from readily available, inexpensive materials, including plywood for the exterior walls, shop-grade pine for flooring, and standard 2 by 4 studs as rafters and trusses. The present owner liked the unpretentious look and affordable cost of those materials and continued their use in the renovation plans.

There were no windows in the original studio, and the roof provided the only source for

natural light. Another problem was limited access, which was confined to a single barn-style sliding door. In addition, more floor space was needed to permit the installation of a kitchen and a bath.

Sliding glass doors were added along one side of the studio to resolve the lighting problem and provide a second entry. The kitchen and bath were built into an 8-foot addition at one end of the original structure. The kitchen was successfully designed to offer maximum efficiency in limited space and, as a result, even includes a dishwasher. Such spacesavers as ceiling hooks for oversize cookware and open shelving on walls over the countertops are not only efficient but attractive as well.

This single room functions smoothly as an entire house because certain activities are

intentionally assigned to specific
areas, such as in the sleeping
alcove. In addition, the total
living space is enlarged
considerably through much of the
year by the surrounding decks
and nearby heated swimming
pool.

This comfortable two-room
cottage was once a commercial
center in Beaver, Arkansas, an
Ozark Mountain community that
boomed and died with the

fortunes of a local limestone quarry. Beaver counted 17 different taverns within its city limits at the turn of the century, including one that was reputedly located in the ground floor of this house. The local doctor had an office upstairs. Some of the old-timers say that the doctor practiced medicine by day and tended the bar at night.

One of Beaver's thirty-three year-round residents lives in the house now, which was bought in 1974 by its present owners for use as a vacation house. A practical, inexpensive renovation was designed to add modern conveniences, yet retain the rustic charm of the ninety-year-old structure.

Both the stone foundation and the upper story were in good structural condition. Once a cedar shake roof was laid over deteriorating asphalt shingles, the owners were able to turn their attention to the two large rooms inside.

The existing interior was gutted on both levels. The ceiling was raised in the main living area to create a greater sense of interior space. A small dormer was added along the south wall and an abstract stained-glass window installed to take advantage of bright afternoon sun and add visual interest to the room. With the addition of natural light and more vertical space, the room was ready for paneling from floor to ceiling with weathered oak barn wood. Then the original oak flooring was refinished and sealed.

New appliances were installed in the kitchen alcove and a thin sheet of copper laid as a countertop around the kitchen sink. New fixtures were installed in the bathroom and an airtight wood stove was set into a central location to provide sufficient year-round heat.

This historic small house is located on a heavily wooded two-acre site that overlooks man-made Table Rock Lake, a scenic body of water some sixty miles long that begins several miles away behind a dam at the headwaters of the White River. The house looks across the narrow lake to steep limestone cliffs that sharply drop over seventy feet into the water. The cliffs are growing brush, small trees, and other forest greenery, but they still serve as a reminder of the former quarrying activity in the days when Beaver was an important center of Ozark Mountain life.

This almost completely remodeled farmhouse conceals a spacious and contemporary interior behind a modest and traditional exterior facade. The owners collaborated with a local builder for several years and designed a thorough renovation of the existing structure, originally built in 1905, to meet their needs for additional living space. The result is an attractive series of large open rooms that make the house seem much larger than its present 1600 square feet.

The house is located near Sebastopol, California, in a small forest of bay trees and native evergreens. Beyond the forest lie 200 continuous acres of apple orchards. The traditional appearance of the original farmhouse was in part preserved with respect for the rural

location.

Remodeling occurred in three separate phases. An existing front porch was enclosed in order to enlarge the bedroom during the first stage and the living/dining room was expanded as well. A year later the kitchen was completely redesigned and rebuilt, and a large family room was added to the house. Finally, a large deck was built across the south wall and an outdoor swimming pool with Jacuzzi outlets was installed.

The owners travel extensively and have furnished the house with many pieces and art from Southeast Asia and Central America, including batik paintings from India, Sri Lanka and Indonesia, brass tables from Bangladesh, and rugs from Nepal and Tibet.

There is considerable visual interest in every room of the house but nothing is quite so dramatic as the twelve-sided stained glass window, nearly five feet in diameter, that is located in the family room. The colorful window was designed and fabricated from imported glass by a local artist and friend of the owners. It provides both decoration and inspiration, as it is often used for meditation.

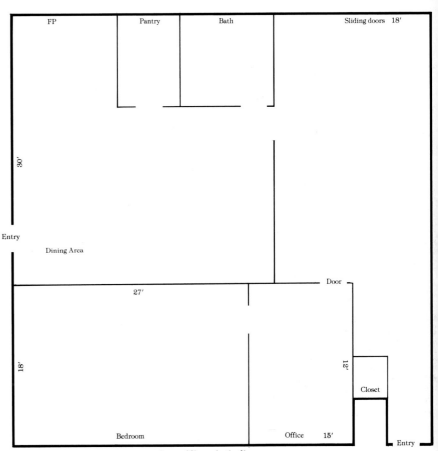

Approx. 48' on each side of house
All measurements very approx.

The imaginative use of color in this converted Victorian firehouse makes this small house in the Ozark Mountains a visual adventure. It is located in Eureka Springs, Arkansas, which was built at the turn of the century as a hot springs resort and today is nationally acclaimed as a community dedicated to the painstaking restoration of its Victorian architectural legacy.

The present owners moved into this house three years ago. They had past experience with extensive restoration of an early-nineteenth-century house in Georgia and did not want to undertake as ambitious or costly an effort again. This one-time firehouse offered sufficient space for the owners and their ten-year-old daughter and simply needed painting and other minor cosmetic work to make it livable.

A bright and bold color scheme was chosen and carried consistently through the house. Even the pine floors, which were original but made with shop-grade lumber, were painted to cover old blemishes. The owner, whose paintings sell at galleries throughout the South, carried her strong eye for color along when she chose the exterior paint.

Ceiling fans were installed in the living room and bedrooms to circulate heat from a central gas-fired furnace in the winter and cool the house during the summer. Each room is large and has a high ceiling, which helps give the entire house a feeling of greater-than-actual space.

A wide veranda, adorned with turned columns and other fancy Victorian millwork, wraps around three sides of the house. The porch serves as protected outdoor living space through the warm months, when it is used for dining, reading, or simply sitting. The surrounding yard has been landscaped with rock gardens, cobblestone paths, and a large teardrop-shaped water lily pond.

The house, which was built in 1906, is furnished with many Victorian pieces that the owners

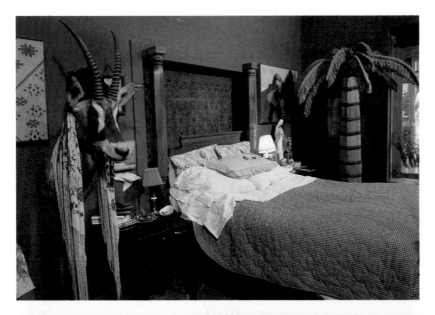

have collected over the last ten years. An assortment of period collectibles, including numerous prints, ceramics, and baskets is combined with such contemporary, Victorian-inspired accents as a hand-woven palm tree.

	16'		6'		18'	
12'	Child's Bedroom		Bath	10'	Kitchen	10'
					20'	
10'	Study		Closet		Dining Room	12'
		17'				
18'	Master Bedroom				Living Room	18'

40' × 40'

Richard and Margaret Storch

This two-story log house was built from second-growth Douglas fir and western red cedar that had covered an acre of government surplus land on Bainbridge Island, Washington. Times were hard in the Pacific Northwest in 1936, and the opportunity to use free building materials to build a house on a low-cost site filled the builder of this cabin with great enthusiasm. The old man, a retired railroad worker who had travelled hundreds of thousands of miles throughout Canada and the United States, was happy to settle down and build his dream house. He went to work on the island near Seattle with little more than a set of basic tools, tireless strength drawn from decades of hard physical labor, and a wealth of common sense.

His design for the house was very simple, but the project took nearly four years to complete. The builder worked alone, felling the trees, peeling and milling the logs, but hired an extra hand or two to help him actually raise the walls. He did all of the interior finish work, plumbing, and wiring by himself and was no doubt filled with pride and satisfaction when the house was finally finished.

He had only been in residence for a few months when World War II began and the decommissioned naval radio station, on whose property the house had been built, was returned to active military status. The log house and several other dwellings on the site had to be moved within sixty days or face

demolition. The builder
purchased a nearby acre lot and
moved the house to its present
location.

The builder's daughter, who
lived in the house for years after
her father died, sold it to the
present owners in 1974 with an
understanding that the rustic
charm and simple design of the
house would always be
maintained. With that condition
in mind, the owners hired an
architect to make the house more
comfortable for their growing
family.

A dining alcove, built with
logs that were matched closely to
the timbers in the original walls,
was added to the main living area.
The enlarged space is drawn
together as a single room with the
addition, in the new area, of oak
flooring, which was also laid over
the original fir floorboards in the
living room. Cedar paneling on
the living area ceiling was
matched and continued into the
new dining space, as were several
large beams. The addition not
only gave the house a formal
eating area but created a
playroom for the owners' two-
year-old daughter and her friends.

There were originally three
very small bedrooms on the
second floor, which the present
owners decided to open into two
larger and more comfortable
sleeping rooms. To supplement
the one small closet upstairs, an
armoire was purchased for
convenient clothes storage in the
master bedroom. That large piece
of furniture made it necessary to
expand the room, and a small
dormer was added. A barber stove

was also installed to provide a convenient source of heat on the second floor.

A large outdoor deck was added to the entry side of the house to facilitate daily use in the spring and summer months of the spacious, informally landscaped yard. Many family activities were comfortably relocated to the deck. It also became a favorite place to entertain large groups of friends.

Low maintenance requirements both inside and outside this house make the owners very happy. The only regular chore is the gradual replacement of the existing chinking between the logs, which originally included newspaper, woven horsehair, and fiberglass, with more permanent plastic foam tubing.

The owners plan to enlarge the 1200-square-foot house as their family grows. An attached sleeping wing with several bedrooms and a second bath may be added or perhaps an entirely separate guest house will be designed and built. But regardless of floor plan, the next addition will surely be built with logs.

The coziness and charm of this small house is enhanced by seven-foot ceilings, a narrow stairway between the first and second floors, and properly scaled furnishings, such as a two-person loveseat in the main living area instead of a large overstuffed couch. This simple log house makes no pretense about its basic design and solid construction. As a result, it is a house of surprising sophistication and lasting substance.

John and Arlene Noble

"We bought this house in 1971 because it felt like an apartment. We had always felt comfortable in a limited amount of living space and wanted our first house to feel as much like home as the apartment that we had just given up." The owners were also attracted to this small California Mission style house, originally built in the late 1920s, for its sweeping view of the San Francisco Bay from its site on the upper slopes of the hills above Berkeley.

The site itself was another advantage of this small house. The lot is pie-shaped and drops sharply from the street toward a ravine. The back of the house

faces due west, which not only ensures spectacular views but maximum natural light throughout the house. In addition, the western exposure allows large windows to admit solar heat passively.

The owners planned to renovate and remodel the house almost as soon as they were unpacked. They began with the kitchen, which still had some of the original fixtures and flooring. Cabinets were replaced, new appliances installed, and a coat of paint and accent wallpaper were put on to brighten the room.

When the kitchen was completed, the owners designed a small deck located just outside

the arched windows of the living room. Then the existing garage was converted into a spacious playroom for their toddler.

By 1975, the owners were ready to redesign this small house to increase the amount of living space or move into a larger house. Its architectural style, excellent view, and possibilities for renovation and addition convinced them to stay in this house. They began several months of consultation with an architect who designed a plan to suit their current and anticipated needs for more space.

A second level was built in the basement underneath the main living area to create a master bedroom and bathroom suite and a large study/living room was added to the dining room. In order to accommodate a stairway to the new level without blocking the view from the living room, the exterior wall was extended four feet. The original wall was preserved because its three graceful arches, the original outside door and companion windows, mirrored the arched front door and windows at the other end of the room.

The spacious master bedroom has an exposed framework of massive redwood beams. The western wall has several large windows that frame the expansive view. An adjoining bath features a sunken bathtub, surrounded with dark blue ceramic tile, accented with red and white decorative pieces. The upper part of the wall between the bedroom and bath is glass, as are the sliding doors that lead out onto the hot-tub deck.

There are three decks on the western side of the house. The lowest one is designed as a children's playground, an important addition to a house with little or no accessible yard. The children's deck is filled with play equipment, including a full-size jungle gym, a basketball backboard and hoop, and a sunken tub filled with sand.

The decks provide not only additional living area for the family but platform gardens where pots and planters full of annual flowers and vegetables can be grown.

The house is surrounded with dense vegetation of blackberry bushes and a few small trees. The trees, both redwood and deciduous, not only shade the decks on hot sunny days but give some privacy from immediate neighbors as well. Privacy is assured in the front of the house by high stucco walls that form a brick courtyard between the house and the street.

"We could only expand the house down the hill, when we considered the shape of the lot. With the additional rooms and decks now completed, we realize that we wouldn't have been happy with any other plan," the owners point out. The 1500-square-foot house is still small, but it is now completely satisfactory.

Jeffrey Milstein, Architect

This no-frills small house, a basic square that is easily constructed with inexpensive materials, was designed and built in 1975 by the architect/owner at the request of a national magazine. Although it was originally designed as an affordable vacation house for a family with several children, the house is a fine primary residence for one or two adults, as the architect/builder can personally attest. He moved into the house after its completion five years ago and has lived there comfortably ever since.

The house is sited in a small clearing on three heavily wooded acres near Woodstock, New York. It rests on poured concrete piers and has painted plywood exterior siding and an asphalt shingle roof. The same austerity of materials characterizes the interior, where trim and other finish details are held to a minimum.

The luxury of this house is found in the spaciousness of the interior plan, which is basically open, and the thoughtful use of expanded vertical space. Large windows on the south and east walls admit maximum natural light, as does a small skylight over the stairwell. Both light and vertical extension are concentrated in the main living area, which is also centered in front of an airtight wood-burning stove.

Although the stove provides the major source of space heat in the house throughout the year, there is a passive solar energy collector at work as well. A concrete mass wall located on the south wall of the house collects solar heat during the day and slowly radiates it into the house at night.

The second level of this very efficient small house has a bedroom that is enclosed for privacy and an office/studio that is open to the living area below. Plastic boxes are used for storage and to support a closet-door-size platform desk. Additional storage space is on several wooden shelves that are hung on brackets and mounted on the wall between the top of the L-shaped desk and the ceiling. The entire space is lighted by aluminum reflector lamps clipped onto a wooden bar that is attached to the ceiling.

A skillful craftsman worked for three months with less than $6000 in building materials to create this small house in an existing two-car garage, built originally in the 1920s in Berkeley. The owners decided to convert the garage to rental property and consulted an architect. He advised them to proceed with the idea because the building was in excellent structural condition. Basic plans were drawn to retain a single open room on the ground floor and open up a small attic underneath the steeply gabled roof for use as a bedroom.

The main living area was divided into locations for daily activity. The kitchen was placed along one entire wall, and a dining area was designed in a corner across the room. A Franklin stove was installed on a country-style brick hearth to provide space heat. A small end wall was lined with a built-in couch.

The owners, who lived in a classic Bay Area Shingle-style house, had a strong appreciation of natural materials and fine craftsmanship. They wanted the hand-crafted appearance of their large house to be continued in the renovated garage. The builder was encouraged to use wood wherever possible. As a result, the small house is rich in redwood paneling, window trim, and shelving that blends well with the oak floors.

The consistent attention to detail throughout this

320-square-foot house resulted in the installation of several panels of antique stained glass, the geometric use of fancy ceramic tile on the countertop that surrounds the kitchen sink, and a stair rail made with a ship's rope.